SCHOLASTIC

Reading Passages
That Build Comprehension

FACT & OPINION

BY LINDA WARD BEECH

D1717034

NEW YORK • TORONTO • LONDON • AUCKLAND • SYDNEY
MEXICO CITY • NEW DELHI • HONG KONG • BUENOS AIRES

Teaching
Resources

Contents

Cover design by Maria Lilja
Interior design by Holly Grundon
Interior art by Mike Gordon

ISBN 0-439-55422-5
Copyright © 2005 by Linda Ward Beech.
All rights reserved.
Printed in the U.S.A.

7 8 9 10   40   14 13 12 11 10

Introduction

Reading comprehension involves numerous thinking skills. Identifying fact and opinion is one such skill. A reader who can differentiate between these two kinds of statements is better able to analyze and assess a text. This book will help you help students learn to identify statements of fact and opinion. Use the pages that follow to teach this skill to students and to give them practice in employing it.

Using This Book

Pages 5-7

After introducing fact and opinion to students (see page 4), duplicate and pass out pages 5–7. Use page 5 to help students review and practice what they have just learned about identifying fact and opinion. By explaining their thinking, students are using metacognition to analyze how they recognized and utilized these clues. Pages 6–7 give students a model of the practice pages to come. They also provide a model of the thinking students might use in distinguishing between facts and opinions.

Page 8

Use this page as a pre-assessment to find out how students think when they identify fact and opinion. When going over these pages with students, discuss how different clues help them decide what kind of statement they read.

Pages 9-43

These pages offer practice in identifying fact and opinion. Students should first read the paragraph, then identify as fact or opinion the selected sentences for the first exercise on the page. The second exercise calls for students to write another fact or opinion from the paragraph. Be sure students understand that the sentence they write should not be one used in the first exercise.

Pages 44-46

After they have completed the practice pages, use these pages to assess the way students think when they identify fact and opinion.

Page 47

You may wish to keep a record of students' progress as they complete the practice pages. Sample comments that will help you guide students toward improving their passages might include:
- reads carelessly
- misunderstands text
- fails to recognize clues
- doesn't apply prior knowledge

Teacher Tip

For students who need extra help, you might suggest that they keep pages 5–7 with them to use as examples when they complete the practice pages.

Mini-Lesson: Teaching About Fact & Opinion

1. Introduce the concept: Write these sentences on the chalkboard:

Most classrooms have desks and chairs.

I think classrooms should have couches.

Ask students which statement can be proved. Which statement is what someone believes?

2. Model thinking: After students have correctly recognized that the first statement can be proved and the second statement is based on belief, continue the lesson by modeling how a student might think aloud.

To show that the first statement is true, I can look around this classroom and others in our school and see desks and chairs. This helps me know that the first statement is a fact.

The second statement tells what I think. Most classrooms don't have couches, but I still think they should. The words *I think* and *should* are clues that this statement is an opinion.

Teacher Tip

Students can learn a lot if you review the finished practice pages with them on a regular basis. Encourage students to explain their thinking for each correct answer. Ask them to point out the words that help them identify facts and opinions. Discuss why the other sentences are not correct choices.

3. Define the skill: Tell students that a **fact** can be proved to be true. Sometimes you can see the proof easily. Sometimes you can look up a fact in a reference source. Facts answer these questions:

• Who? • What? • Where? • When? • Why? • How?

Tell students that books such as encyclopedias, almanacs, textbooks, biographies, and other nonfiction books all contain facts. So do newspapers and news magazines.

Explain that an **opinion** may or may not be true. An opinion is what someone thinks or believes. An opinion is a kind of judgment. There may be many opinions about a subject. Opinions can be based on facts, or they can be based on feelings. Sometimes they are based on both. Sometimes statements of opinion have clues in them that help a reader identify them.

• *I think; I believe; I feel; in my opinion*
• phrases using words such as *best, should, better than, must*

Caution students that not all opinions have these clue words. Opinions can also be given like this:

Couches are a great idea for classrooms.

Explain that opinions are found in many kinds of reading material. Advertisements are opinions. Many magazines and newspapers carry features that offer the writer's opinion. The editorial page of a newspaper is set aside for opinions.

What Is a Fact? What Is an Opinion?

You read a paragraph. It gives you a lot of information. But you aren't sure it's all true. And you don't agree with everything you have read. What can you do? A good reader sorts out the information. A reader might think:

Which statements can be proved?

Which statements are what the writer thinks?

When you answer the first question, you identify the **facts**. The facts are statements that can be proved true. When you answer the second question, you identify **opinions**. An opinion is what someone thinks or believes.

Read the paragraph below, and then answer the questions.

Dogs Around the World

Most dogs are pets. But there are still wild dogs in different parts of the world. I think the jackal—found in Africa, Asia, and Europe—is the most dangerous. In Australia, the dingo is a native wild dog. Another wild dog is the coyote in North America.

What facts are given in this paragraph?

1. Who or what is the paragraph about?

   _____

2. What are some examples of these animals?

   _____

3. Where are some of these animals found?

   _____

What opinion is given?

4. What judgment does the writer make about jackals?

   _____

5. How could you prove that the facts are true?

   _____

Name _____ Date _____

Identifying Facts & Opinions

Study these two pages. They show how a student identified facts and opinions.

Read the paragraph. Then answer the questions.

Outdoor Movies

The best way to see a movie is at a drive-in theater. These outdoor theaters had their beginnings in 1933 in Riverton, New Jersey. Richard Hollingshead, Jr., set up a movie screen in front of his garage. Later that year he opened a real drive-in theater in the town of Camden. This theater had room for 400 cars. What a clever idea!

---

1. Write *fact* or *opinion* next to each sentence.

_____fact_____ A. This movie theater had room for 400 cars.

This statement can be checked so it must be a **fact**.

Continued ➔

Identifying Facts & Opinions

(Continued)

___opinion___ **B. The best way to see a movie is at a drive-in theater.**

This sentence tells what the writer thinks. You can't prove it is true. I don't even agree with it. It is an **opinion**.

___fact___ **C. These outdoor theaters had their beginnings in 1933 in Riverton, New Jersey.**

This statement tells when and where. It can be proved. It is a **fact**.

2. Write another opinion from the paragraph.

The third and fourth sentences are facts. They can be proved. But the last sentence gives a judgment. It is an opinion. I will write that sentence: *What a clever idea!*

Name_____ Date_____

Sorting Information

Study the picture. Read each sentence. Write **F** if the sentence is a fact.
Write **O** if the sentence is an opinion.

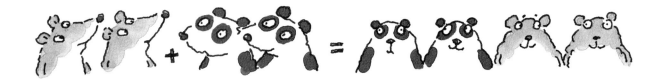

_____ **1.** There are two pandas.

_____ **2.** The pandas are cuter than the brown bears.

_____ **3.** Two plus two equals four.

_____ **4.** There are two bears.

_____ **5.** The artist should have drawn polar bears.

6. Write another fact about the picture.

_____

_____

7. Write another opinion about the picture.

_____

_____

8

Practice Page 1

Name_____ Date_____

Read the paragraph. Then follow the directions.

Classroom Pets

Many classrooms have pets. This is the best way for students to learn about animals. But classroom pets need a place to go during the summer. In Plano, Texas, the schools have a mini-zoo. Teachers can borrow pets for the school months. When summer comes, they return the pets to the zoo. Schools in other towns should follow this example.

1. Write *fact* or *opinion* next to each sentence.

   _____ A. This is the best way for students to learn about animals.

   _____ B. In Plano, Texas, the schools have a mini-zoo.

   _____ C. Schools in other towns should follow this example.

2. Write another fact from the paragraph.

   _____

   _____

   _____

Name_____ Date_____

Read the paragraph. Then follow the directions.

Talking on Trains

Some railroad trains have quiet cars. This means that talking on cell phones is not allowed. It's a great rule. Many people are tired after working all day. They don't care to hear someone else's conversation. People who blab away on cell phones are really rude. Under the cell phone rule, people who do need to talk sit in cars where phones are allowed.

1. **Write *fact* or *opinion* next to each sentence.**

   _____ A. Some railroad trains have quiet cars.

   _____ B. It's a great rule.

   _____ C. Many people are tired after working all day.

2. **Write another opinion from the paragraph.**

   _____

   _____

   _____

Practice Page 3   Name_____   Date_____

Read the paragraph. Then follow the directions.

Nesting Dolls

Nesting dolls are sets of wooden dolls. I think they are very cute. You twist open each doll to find another, smaller doll inside. These dolls were first made in Russia in 1890. Today major league baseball teams are handing out these dolls. They are called Stackable Stars. Each doll is painted to look like a player on the team. Many fans collect the dolls.

1. **Write *fact* or *opinion* next to each sentence.**

   _____ A. I think they are very cute.

   _____ B. Today major league baseball teams are handing out these dolls.

   _____ C. Many fans collect the dolls.

2. **Write another fact from the paragraph.**

   _____

   _____

   _____

Practice Page 4 Name_____ Date_____

Read the paragraph. Then follow the directions.

An Unusual Race

Many places have boat races. But the town of Rieti in Italy has a washtub race. What a silly event! The race takes place on the Velino River. The racers, all men, kneel in the tubs. They use oars to paddle. If a racer isn't careful, the tub tips over. Also, if a racer doesn't paddle correctly, the tub spins around. In my opinion, you have to be a good sport for this race.

1. **Write *fact* or *opinion* next to each sentence.**

   _____ A. The race takes place on the Velino River.

   _____ B. What a silly event!

   _____ C. The racers, all men, kneel in the tubs.

2. **Write another opinion from the paragraph.**

   _____

   _____

   _____

Practice Page 5 **Name**_____ **Date**_____

Read the paragraph. Then follow the directions.

White Rhinos

One of the most amazing sights at a zoo is the white rhino. This animal is quite rare. It is the largest of the five kinds of rhinos. Zookeepers report that white rhinos like spaces that are dry and dusty. They must be rather messy animals. In the wild, the white rhino is a target of hunters. They kill these rhinos for their horns. That's horrible!

1. Write *fact* or *opinion* next to each sentence.

   _____ A. It is the largest of the five kinds of rhinos.

   _____ B. One of the most amazing sights at a zoo is the white rhino.

   _____ C. That's horrible!

2. Write another opinion from the paragraph.

   _____

   _____

   _____

Practice Page 6 *Name*_____ *Date*_____

Read the paragraph. Then follow the directions.

Meet Norman Rockwell

Norman Rockwell was a famous American artist. He was one of the best artists the country has ever seen. Many of Rockwell's paintings appeared on the cover of a magazine. It was called the *Saturday Evening Post.* Rockwell painted all kinds of pictures. When he painted scenes with lots of people, he sometimes ran out of models. Then he painted himself into the picture.

1. Write *fact* or *opinion* next to each sentence.

   _____ A. Many of Rockwell's paintings appeared on the cover of a magazine.

   _____ B. He was one of the best artists the country has ever seen.

   _____ C. Then he painted himself into the picture.

2. Write another fact from the paragraph.

   _____

   _____

   _____

Name_____ Date_____

Read the paragraph. Then follow the directions.

Crossing the Delaware

Everyone should know this story. In 1776 George Washington was leading the American army against England. The night of December 24 was bitter cold. Snow and sleet were falling. Sleet is the worst kind of weather. Washington and his men were on one side of the Delaware River. During the night they crossed the icy waters. They snuck up on the enemy and beat them in a big battle.

1. Write *fact* or *opinion* next to each sentence.

   _____ A. Everyone should know this story.

   _____ B. In 1776 George Washington was leading the American army against England.

   _____ C. During the night they crossed the icy waters.

2. Write another opinion from the paragraph.

   _____

   _____

   _____

Name_____ Date_____

Read the paragraph. Then follow the directions.

Word Stories

Thomas Blanket sold woolen goods long ago in England. The English word *blanket* comes from his name. A cloth called calico is named after Calicut. This is a town in India where cotton cloth was made. You should always know where words come from. It's the best way to impress people.

1. **Write *fact* or *opinion* next to each sentence.**

   _____ A. A cloth called calico is named after Calicut.

   _____ B. The English word *blanket* comes from his name.

   _____ C. You should always know where words come from.

2. **Write another opinion from the paragraph.**

   _____

   _____

   _____

Practice Page **9**

Name_____ Date_____

Read the paragraph. Then follow the directions.

Big Cat

The jaguar is one of the four big cats. The others are lions, tigers, and leopards. Jaguars live in warm climates in Latin America. They are the most beautiful of all wild cats. A jaguar has a big head and a strong jaw. Its paws and claws are huge. The jaguar is a silent and deadly hunter. However, it rarely attacks people. The jaguar spends most of its time alone and even stays away from other jaguars.

1. **Write _fact_ or _opinion_ next to each sentence.**

   _____ A. The jaguar is one of the four big cats.

   _____ B. Jaguars live in warm climates in Latin America.

   _____ C. They are the most beautiful of all wild cats.

2. **Write another fact from the paragraph.**

   _____

   _____

   _____

Practice Page 10 Name_____ Date_____

Read the paragraph. Then follow the directions.

An Interesting Artist

M. C. Escher was a Dutch artist. I think he had a really amazing mind. He must have been an interesting person. Some of Escher's works are like math puzzles. They show repeating patterns and designs. Escher also drew pictures that tease the viewer. Some of these have paths and staircases that go nowhere. I feel that his work is fun to look at.

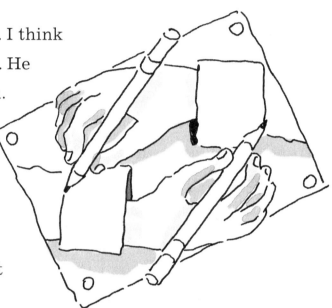

1. **Write *fact* or *opinion* next to each sentence.**

   _____ A. He must have been an interesting person.

   _____ B. Some of Escher's works are like math puzzles.

   _____ C. I feel that his work is fun to look at.

2. **Write another fact from the paragraph.**

   _____

   _____

   _____

Practice Page 11 **Name**_____ **Date**_____

Read the paragraph. Then follow the directions.

In a Fog

The worst thing for a driver is fog. In some parts of the country, fog causes accidents on highways. In 2003, 73 cars crashed during a foggy weekend in Maryland. In some places roads are closed when it is foggy. Other places have special signs that can sense fog. When there is a fog alert, the signs change to lower the speed limit. Drivers shouldn't go out in fog, if you ask me.

1. **Write _fact_ or _opinion_ next to each sentence.**

   _____ A. The worst thing for a driver is fog.

   _____ B. In some places roads are closed when it is foggy.

   _____ C. Drivers shouldn't go out in fog, if you ask me.

2. **Write another fact from the paragraph.**

   _____

   _____

   _____

Practice Page **12**

Name_____ Date_____

Read the paragraph. Then follow the directions.

Some Soup!

Birds called swifts are popular in Thailand. People there welcome the birds into their homes. In one city the birds even live in a hotel. The reason the birds are in such demand is their nests. Bird's nest soup is a big treat in Thailand. I don't think I would care for it. Vegetable soup seems better to me!

1. **Write *fact* or *opinion* next to each sentence.**

   _____ A. Birds called swifts are popular in Thailand.

   _____ B. I don't think I would care for it.

   _____ C. In one city the birds even live in a hotel.

2. **Write another opinion from the paragraph.**

   _____

   _____

   _____

Name_____ Date_____

Read the paragraph. Then follow the directions.

Family Fun Long Ago

People in ancient Egypt weren't lucky enough to have televisions or computers. They spent their free time in other ways. Families often went on outings along the Nile River. Sometimes they sailed in boats. Often the children caught fish with spears or nets. They also picked flowers that grew along the shores. Children today have a lot more fun.

1. **Write *fact* or *opinion* next to each sentence.**

   _____ A. Families often went on outings along the Nile River.

   _____ B. Children today have a lot more fun.

   _____ C. Often the children caught fish with spears or nets.

2. **Write another fact from the paragraph.**

   _____

   _____

   _____

Name_____ Date_____

Read the paragraph. Then follow the directions.

Where Chess Is Big

In North Carolina an artist makes huge chess sets. The sets take up most of a backyard. The pieces are made from "found" materials, usually metal. Each piece is fabulous! To play the game, people walk around on the board. When they are ready to move, they have to push or pull the pieces. This must be the most fun way to play chess.

1. **Write *fact* or *opinion* next to each sentence.**

   _____ A. In North Carolina an artist makes huge chess sets.

   _____ B. To play the game, people walk around on the board.

   _____ C. Each piece is fabulous!

2. **Write another opinion from the paragraph.**

   _____

   _____

   _____

Practice Page 15

Name_____   Date_____

Read the paragraph. Then follow the directions.

Silly Laws

Some laws are really stupid. In Idaho you can get in trouble if you fish from a camel's back. That's ridiculous! In Arizona there's a fine if you let a donkey fall asleep in your bathtub. That's just silly. In Vermont it's against the law to whistle underwater. And a city in Minnesota has a law forbidding people to drive red cars.

1. **Write *fact* or *opinion* next to each sentence.**

   _____ A. Some laws are really stupid.

   _____ B. In Arizona there's a fine if you let a donkey fall asleep
   in your bathtub.

   _____ C. That's ridiculous!

2. **Write another fact from the paragraph.**

   _____

   _____

   _____

Practice Page 16 Name_____ Date_____

Read the paragraph. Then follow the directions.

In the Deep

Scientists use special machines to make maps of the ocean floor. They send sound waves down to measure how deep each spot is. They can also use satellite information to make computer pictures. They have found that Earth's highest mountain range is underwater. There are also volcanoes, slopes, flat areas, and much more. The bottom of the ocean is so interesting.

1. **Write *fact* or *opinion* next to each sentence.**

   _____ A. Scientists use special machines to make maps of the ocean floor.

   _____ B. The bottom of the ocean is so interesting.

   _____ C. There are also volcanoes, slopes, flat areas, and much more.

2. **Write another fact from the paragraph.**

   _____

   _____

   _____

Practice Page 17   Name_____   Date_____

Read the paragraph. Then follow the directions.

Staying Warm

Everyone should learn about the animals of the Arctic. These animals are super. They have special ways of living in the cold. For example, the musk ox has two layers of fur. The inner layer traps air warmed by the animal's body. The outer layer has long hairs that protect the ox from wind and water. What a great way to stay warm!

1. Write *fact* or *opinion* next to each sentence.

   _____ A. Everyone should learn about the animals of the Arctic.

   _____ B. What a great way to stay warm!

   _____ C. The inner layer traps air warmed by the animal's body.

2. Write another opinion from the paragraph.

   _____

   _____

   _____

Practice Page 18 **Name**_____ **Date**_____

Read the paragraph. Then answer the questions.

Early Train Rides

The first railroad cars were scary. In the 1830s passengers rode in cars that looked like stagecoaches. Often showers of sparks from the engine blew back on them. That is so unsafe! The crew on these early trains didn't even ride inside a car. If it rained or snowed, they just got wet. I would not have worked on one of these trains.

1. **Write *fact* or *opinion* next to each sentence.**

   _____ A. The first railroad cars were scary.

   _____ B. That is so unsafe!

   _____ C. The crew on these early trains didn't even ride inside a car.

2. **Write another opinion from the paragraph.**

   _____

   _____

   _____

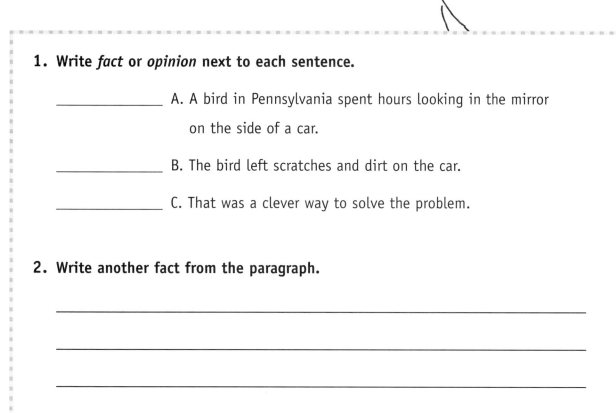

Practice Page 19   Name_____   Date_____

Read the paragraph. Then follow the directions.

A Bird Story

Sometimes birds do unusual things. A bird in Pennsylvania spent hours looking in the mirror on the side of a car. Maybe it wasn't a very smart bird. The bird left scratches and dirt on the car. So the owner put a bag over the mirror when the car was parked. That was a clever way to solve the problem.

1. **Write *fact* or *opinion* next to each sentence.**

   _____ A. A bird in Pennsylvania spent hours looking in the mirror
   on the side of a car.

   _____ B. The bird left scratches and dirt on the car.

   _____ C. That was a clever way to solve the problem.

2. **Write another fact from the paragraph.**

   _____

   _____

   _____

Practice Page 20   Name_____   Date_____

Read the paragraph. Then follow the directions.

Gray Whales

Gray whales spend their winters in warm waters off Mexico. I think that's very smart of them. The females have their young and nurse them during this time. By late spring the whales begin swimming north. They travel about 5,000 miles to the waters of the Arctic. These are their feeding grounds. They eat tiny creatures that look like shrimp. Gray whales are really amazing.

1. **Write *fact* or *opinion* next to each sentence.**

   _____ A. I think that's very smart of them.

   _____ B. The females have their young and nurse them during this time.

   _____ C. They travel about 5,000 miles to the waters of the Arctic.

2. **Write another opinion from the paragraph.**

   _____

   _____

   _____

Practice Page 21 | Name_____ Date_____

Read the paragraph. Then follow the directions.

Names on the Map

You can find girls' first names on maps of Georgia. It's quite amusing. You'll find towns with names such as Lilly or Helen. You'll also find towns called Cornelia and Roberta. Kathleen just doesn't seem like a town name. Edith is okay for a girl but not for a town. In Georgia you can also visit the communities of Daisy, Lula, and Rebecca.

1. Write *fact* or *opinion* next to each sentence.

   _____ A. It's quite amusing.

   _____ B. Kathleen just doesn't seem like a town name.

   _____ C. You'll find towns with names such as Lilly or Helen.

2. Write another opinion from the paragraph.

   _____

   _____

   _____

Practice Page 22

Name_____ Date_____

Read the paragraph. Then follow the directions.

In the Shell

When a chick is in its shell, it needs air to breathe. The air seeps through tiny holes in the shell. Then the air passes through a thin skin inside the shell. Blood vessels carry the air to the chick. At one end of the shell is an air bubble. When the chick is ready to hatch, it pops this bubble. Then it practices using its lungs to breathe. Chicks look funny when they hatch.

1. Write *fact* or *opinion* next to each sentence.

_____ A. The air seeps through tiny holes in the shell.

_____ B. Blood vessels carry the air to the chick.

_____ C. Chicks look funny when they hatch.

2. Write another fact from the paragraph.

_____

_____

_____

Practice Page **23**   Name_____   Date_____

Read the paragraph. Then follow the directions.

Different Customs

People in other lands have some strange customs. I would like to live in South Korea. It's good manners to slurp soup there. I think slurping soup shows that you like it. My mother says it is impolite. In South Korea it is also good manners to burp. I love the idea. A good slurp and a good burp are fine with me.

1. **Write *fact* or *opinion* next to each sentence.**

   _____ A. I would like to live in South Korea.

   _____ B. It's good manners to slurp soup there.

   _____ C. I think slurping soup shows that you like it.

2. **Write another opinion from the paragraph.**

   _____

   _____

   _____

Practice Page 24 Name_____ Date_____

Read the paragraph. Then follow the directions.

The Appalachian Trail

Everyone wants to walk on the Appalachian Trail. This path is 2,160 miles long. It goes from Katahdin, Maine, to Springer Mountain, Georgia. Some hikers walk the whole trail. Others follow it for a few hours or a day. The most annoying people on the trail are noisy teens. They should stay at home. However, most people walk along and enjoy the birds, animals, and plants.

1. **Write *fact* or *opinion* next to each sentence.**

    _____ A. Everyone wants to walk on the Appalachian Trail.

    _____ B. This path is 2,160 miles long.

    _____ C. The most annoying people on the trail are noisy teens.

2. **Write another opinion from the paragraph.**

    _____

    _____

    _____

Practice Page **25**

Name_____ **Date**_____

Read the paragraph. Then follow the directions.

Pilgrim Food

Pilgrims didn't have refrigerators. They had other ways to keep food from going bad. To keep meat fresh, they stored it in barrels of salt. Salty food doesn't taste very good. The Pilgrims hung vegetables and fruits up to dry them. They put some foods like turnips and carrots in cool places to keep them fresh. They also buried eggs in straw. I think our meals are more tasty than what the Pilgrims ate.

1. **Write *fact* or *opinion* next to each sentence.**

   _____ A. Pilgrims didn't have refrigerators.

   _____ B. To keep meat fresh, they stored it in barrels of salt.

   _____ C. Salty food doesn't taste very good.

2. **Write another fact from the paragraph.**

   _____

   _____

   _____

Practice Page 26 Name_____ Date_____

Read the paragraph. Then follow the directions.

Cloth for Clothes

People wear clothes made of cotton, wool, silk, and many other materials. Silk is the best. Now a scientist has invented cloth with tiny wires in it. This cloth can pick up signals from the wearer's body. I think this is very exciting. For example, the cloth can tell what a person's temperature is. If the wearer is sick, the cloth can send a signal to a computer to call for help.

1. **Write *fact* or *opinion* next to each sentence.**

   _____ A. Silk is the best.

   _____ B. Now a scientist has invented cloth with tiny wires in it.

   _____ C. This cloth can pick up signals from the wearer's body.

2. **Write another opinion from the paragraph.**

   _____

   _____

   _____

Reading Passages That Build Comprehension: Fact & Opinion   Scholastic Teaching Resources

Practice Page 27   Name_____   Date_____

Read the paragraph. Then follow the directions.

State of Good Food

Rhode Island is the best state for good food. Eating there is so much fun. If you want a milkshake, you have to order a cabinet. That's the name it's called in Rhode Island. Many places sell coffee milk. This is a drink like chocolate milk that is made with coffee syrup. It's yummy. For breakfast Rhode Islanders eat johnnycakes. These are pancakes made with cornmeal.

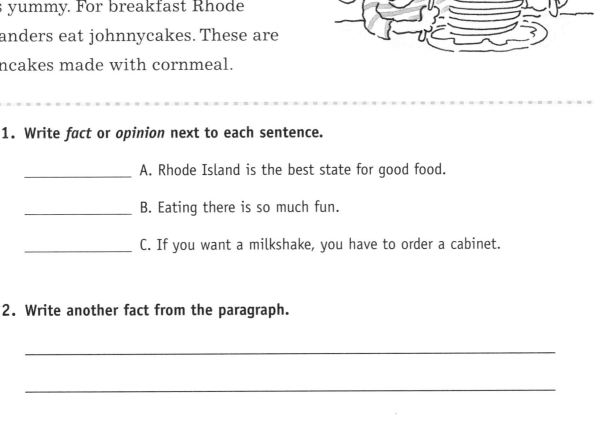

1. **Write *fact* or *opinion* next to each sentence.**

_____ A. Rhode Island is the best state for good food.

_____ B. Eating there is so much fun.

_____ C. If you want a milkshake, you have to order a cabinet.

2. **Write another fact from the paragraph.**

_____

_____

_____

Practice Page **28** Name_____ Date_____

Read the paragraph. Then follow the directions.

Measure by Measure

People and horses are measured for height in different ways. People are measured from head to toe. But horses move their heads up and down a lot. It is hard to get a fixed measurement. So horses are measured from their feet to their withers. The withers are on a horse's back above the shoulders. You should remember this to tell your friends.

1. **Write *fact* or *opinion* next to each sentence.**

   _____ A. People are measured from head to toe.

   _____ B. But horses move their heads up and down a lot.

   _____ C. You should remember this to tell your friends.

2. **Write another fact from the paragraph.**

   _____

   _____

   _____

Practice Page **29** Name_____ Date_____

Read the paragraph. Then follow the directions.

Home Plate

nce, home plate on a baseball field was square. Then, in 1900, the shape was changed. Since then home plate has had five sides. That's so weird. The reason for this change was to help umpires. They find it easier to see the ball with this five-sided shape. It seems to me they still have trouble seeing the ball at times. I think the players also have problems.

---

1. **Write *fact* or *opinion* next to each sentence.**

   _____ A. Once, home plate on a baseball field was square.

   _____ B. That's so weird.

   _____ C. It seems to me they still have trouble seeing the ball at times.

2. **Write another opinion from the paragraph.**

   _____

   _____

   _____

Name_____ Date_____

Read the paragraph. Then follow the directions.

Pig Tails

Pigs are known for having curly tails. They're so cute! Experts say that you can tell how healthy a pig is by the curl of its tail. A pig with a curly tail is in good health. But a pig with a straight tail is not. Poor pig. A straight tail on a pig is a sign of illness. Farmers should take good care of their pigs so they don't get sick.

---

1. **Write *fact* or *opinion* next to each sentence.**

   _____ A. They're so cute!

   _____ B. Experts say that you can tell how healthy a pig
   is by the curl of its tail.

   _____ C. A straight tail on a pig is a sign of illness.

2. **Write another opinion from the paragraph.**

   _____

   _____

   _____

Practice Page 31

Name_____ Date_____

Read the paragraph. Then follow the directions.

The Marriage Month

June is the most popular month for weddings. I think September is a better month. June is named for the Roman goddess Juno. Stories say that she took an interest in couples who got married in June. Another reason June may be popular is that long-ago people thought May was an unlucky month. That is a silly idea. May is such a pretty month.

1. **Write *fact* or *opinion* next to each sentence.**

   _____ A. June is the most popular month for weddings.

   _____ B. I think September is a better month.

   _____ C. That is a silly idea.

2. **Write another fact from the paragraph.**

   _____

   _____

   _____

Practice Page 32   Name_____ Date_____

Read the paragraph. Then follow the directions.

Firehouse Dogs

Dalmatians are known as firehouse dogs. They are wonderful dogs. They are fast and have good memories. Dalmatians also get along well with horses. Long ago, fire trucks were pulled by horses. Firefighters used dalmatians to run ahead of the trucks and clear a path. Today some firehouses still keep a dalmatian. They no longer have to run ahead of horses, though.

---

1. Write *fact* or *opinion* next to each sentence.

_____ A. Dalmatians are known as firehouse dogs.

_____ B. Long ago, fire trucks were pulled by horses.

_____ C. They are wonderful dogs.

2. Write another fact from the paragraph.

_____

_____

_____

Name_____ Date_____

Read the paragraph. Then follow the directions.

Meet the Marsupials

Some animals carry their young in a pouch. These animals are called marsupials. A kangaroo is an example. Another marsupial is the koala. It looks like a little bear. I would love to have one as a pet. I think a kangaroo might be hard to keep at home. Still another marsupial is the wombat. That's a funny name! The wombat looks something like a badger.

1. Write *fact* or *opinion* next to each sentence.

_____ A. Some animals carry their young in a pouch.

_____ B. These animals are called marsupials.

_____ C. I would love to have one as a pet.

2. Write another opinion from the paragraph.

_____

_____

_____

Practice Page 34   Name_____   Date_____

Read the paragraph. Then follow the directions.

Ant Trails

People often come across ants on sidewalks. Scientists say that there is a reason for this. People tend to drop food and food wrappers on sidewalks. These people are slobs. They should know better. Ants are always looking for food. If a scout ant finds food on a sidewalk, it leaves a trail for other ants. Soon there are lots of ants following the trail.

1. **Write *fact* or *opinion* next to each sentence.**

    _____ A. These people are slobs.

    _____ B. People tend to drop food and food wrappers on sidewalks.

    _____ C. They should know better.

2. **Write another fact from the paragraph.**

    _____

    _____

    _____

Practice Page 35   Name_____ Date_____

Read the paragraph. Then follow the directions.

The Sign of X

Long ago, people used X to sign their names. Some people used X because they didn't know how to read or write. But people also used X as a sign of good faith. Even kings and queens used it. The letter X came to mean that something was legal. Often people kissed the X after writing it. Today an X still means a kiss. Everyone should send Xs to someone.

1. **Write *fact* or *opinion* next to each sentence.**

   _____ A. Some people used X because they didn't know how to read or write.

   _____ B. Everyone should send Xs to someone.

   _____ C. The letter X came to mean that something was legal.

2. **Write another fact from the paragraph.**

   _____

   _____

   _____

Assessment 1   Name_____   Date_____

Read the sentences. Some are facts, and some are opinions.
If a sentence is under the wrong heading, put an **X** on the line.

Facts

_____ **1.** Most dogs walk in circles before they lie down.

_____ **2.** They look funny when they do this.

_____ **3.** Dogs circle to map out territory.

_____ **4.** Wild dogs prepare a sleeping place this way.

_____ **5.** Pet dogs should have warm beds.

_____ **6.** Sometimes a dog flattens down tall grass.

Opinions

_____ **7.** Puppies are the cutest animals in the world.

_____ **8.** Mother dogs circle to spread their scent for newborn puppies.

_____ **9.** Everyone should have a pet dog.

_____ **10.** Sometimes dogs turn in circles when they chase their tails.

_____ **11.** Dogs make better pets than cats.

_____ **12.** People must be kind to dogs.

Name _____ Date _____

Read the sentences. Some are facts, and some are opinions.
If a sentence is under the wrong heading, put an **X** on the line.

Facts

_____ **1.** Eggs are not all the same color.

_____ **2.** Some eggs are white, and some are brown.

_____ **3.** People buy more white eggs than any other color.

_____ **4.** I think brown eggs are great.

_____ **5.** The earlobes of a hen tell what color eggs it will lay.

_____ **6.** If a hen has red earlobes, she will lay brown eggs.

Opinions

_____ **7.** People should buy all colors of eggs.

_____ **8.** White earlobes on a hen mean it will lay white eggs.

_____ **9.** Fried eggs taste better than scrambled eggs.

_____ **10.** The color of an egg comes from its outer shell.

_____ **11.** Most white eggs come from hens called Leghorns.

_____ **12.** Everyone should eat lots of eggs.

Assessment 3

Name_____ Date_____

Read the sentences. Some are facts, and some are opinions.
If a sentence is under the wrong heading, put an **X** on the line.

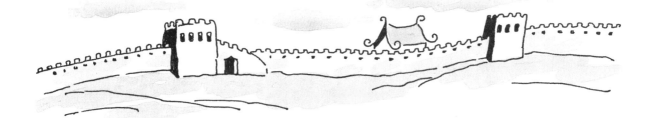

Facts

_____ **1.** The Great Wall of China took hundreds of years to build.

_____ **2.** It stretches about 4,000 miles.

_____ **3.** Everyone should go to see it.

_____ **4.** The wall goes over mountains, deserts, and plains.

_____ **5.** The wall must be kept in good repair.

_____ **6.** There are more than 24,000 gates and towers on the wall.

Opinions

_____ **7.** Students should learn about the Great Wall in school.

_____ **8.** Many workers died while building the wall.

_____ **9.** Other countries should also build great walls.

_____ **10.** Walls are the best way to keep a country safe.

_____ **11.** Parts of the wall have fallen over time.

_____ **12.** I think the wall is one of the best things in China.

Student Record Sheet

Name _____ Date _____

Date	Practice Page # ____	Number Correct	Comments

Answers

Page 5:
1. wild dogs
2. jackal, dingo, coyote
3. Africa, Asia, Europe, Australia, North America
4. The jackal is the most dangerous.
5. Check an encyclopedia or another reference book.

Page 8:
1. F
2. O
3. F
4. F
5. O
6. Possible answer: The bears are shown first.
7. Possible answer: The bears are cute.

Page 9:
1. A. opinion
   B. fact
   C. opinion
2. Possible answer: Many classrooms have pets.

Page 10:
1. A. fact
   B. opinion
   C. fact
2. People who blab away on cell phones are really rude.

Page 11:
1. A. opinion
   B. fact
   C. fact
2. Possible answer: Nesting dolls are sets of wooden dolls.

Page 12:
1. A. fact
   B. opinion
   C. fact
2. In my opinion, you have to be a good sport for this race.

Page 13:
1. A. fact
   B. opinion
   C. opinion
2. They must be rather messy animals.

Page 14:
1. A. fact
   B. opinion
   C. fact
2. Possible answer: It was called the *Saturday Evening Post.*

Page 15:
1. A. opinion
   B. fact
   C. fact
2. Sleet is the worst kind of weather.

Page 16:
1. A. fact
   B. fact
   C. opinion
2. It's the best way to impress people.

Page 17:
1. A. fact
   B. fact
   C. opinion
2. Possible answer: The others are lions, tigers, and leopards.

Page 18:
1. A. opinion
   B. fact
   C. opinion
2. Possible answer: M. C. Escher was a Dutch artist.

Page 19:
1. A. opinion
   B. fact
   C. opinion
2. Possible answer: In 2003, 73 cars crashed during a foggy weekend in Maryland.

Page 20:
1. A. fact
   B. opinion
   C. fact
2. Vegetable soup seems better to me!

Page 21:
1. A. fact
   B. opinion
   C. fact
2. Possible answer: Sometimes they sailed in boats.

Page 22:
1. A. fact
   B. fact
   C. opinion
2. This must be the most fun way to play chess.

Page 23:
1. A. opinion
   B. fact
   C. opinion
2. Possible answer: In Idaho you can get in trouble if you fish from a camel's back.

Page 24:
1. A. fact
   B. opinion
   C. fact
2. Possible answer: They send sound waves down to measure how deep each spot is.

Page 25:
1. A. opinion
   B. opinion
   C. fact
2. These animals are super.

Page 26:
1. A. opinion
   B. opinion
   C. fact
2. I would not have worked on one of these trains.

Page 27:
1. A. fact
   B. fact
   C. opinion
2. Possible answer: Sometimes birds do unusual things.

Page 28:
1. A. opinion
   B. fact
   C. fact
2. Gray whales are really amazing.

Page 29:
1. A. opinion
   B. opinion
   C. fact
2. Edith is okay for a girl but not for a town.

Page 30:
1. A. fact
   B. fact
   C. opinion
2. Possible answer: When a chick is in its shell, it needs air to breathe.

Page 31:
1. A. opinion
   B. fact
   C. opinion
2. Possible answer: People in other lands have some strange customs.

Page 32:
1. A. opinion
   B. fact
   C. opinion
2. Possible answer: They should stay at home.

Page 33:
1. A. fact
   B. fact
   C. opinion
2. Possible answer: They had other ways to keep food from going bad.

Page 34:
1. A. opinion
   B. fact
   C. fact
2. I think this is very exciting.

Page 35:
1. A. opinion
   B. opinion
   C. fact
2. Possible answer: Many places sell coffee milk.

Page 36:
1. A. fact
   B. fact
   C. opinion
2. Possible answer: People and horses are measured for height in different ways.

Page 37:
1. A. fact
   B. opinion
   C. opinion
2. I think the players also have problems.

Page 38:
1. A. opinion
   B. fact
   C. fact
2. Possible answer: Poor pig.

Page 39:
1. A. fact
   B. opinion
   C. opinion
2. Possible answer: June is named for the Roman goddess Juno.

Page 40:
1. A. fact
   B. fact
   C. opinion
2. Possible answer: Firefighters used dalmatians to run ahead of the trucks and clear a path.

Page 41:
1. A. fact
   B. fact
   C. opinion
2. Possible answer: I think a kangaroo might be hard to keep at home.

Page 42:
1. A. opinion
   B. fact
   C. opinion
2. Possible answer: People often come across ants on sidewalks.

Page 43:
1. A. fact
   B. opinion
   C. fact
2. Possible answer: Long ago, people used X to sign their names.

Page 44:
Students should put an "X" on: 2, 5, 8, and 11.

Page 45:
Students should put an "X" on: 4, 8, 10, and 11.

Page 46:
Students should put an "X" on: 3, 5, 8, and 11.